The American Coma

ISBN: 1-4820-4454-4
ISBN-13: 9781482044546

The American Coma

A Citizen Awakes

Barbara Norton

2013

Dedication

To my daughter, nieces, and nephew with all my love

They all have kind and generous hearts and brilliant minds. They will make the world a better place.

TABLE OF CONTENTS

Introduction

Sleeping minds are making dangerous decisions. A lack of rational thinking is causing us to make decisions and choices that do not give us positive results. Many of us are allowing our emotional minds to rule our lives. This leaves us vulnerable to those who take advantage of our sleeping state for their own selfish reasons. This is the American Coma and it is leading our country down a dangerous path.

Many of us continue to hold an emotional opinion even when facts and evidence completely refute it. We insist we are right. Some of us resort to name calling, emotional rants, and reciting sound bites to dismiss anyone who disagrees. We have closed off all dialogue and are open only to affirmation of our own locked-in views.

Some of us are intelligent and likeable. Some are arrogant and condescending. What sleeping minds have in common is dealing with certain issues, particularly political issues, from an emotional point of view.

I have been wondering why more and more of us embrace this approach to life. It is a puzzle because, if you watch for awhile, it is clear that this emotional approach isn't very successful. Yet it persists.

The American Coma is spreading across our country. Emotional feelings are explored, developed, and used as a guide to make decisions. The rational brain goes to sleep from lack of development and use. Parents are teaching this approach to their children. Teachers are passing it on to their students. Journalist, filmmakers, judges, and politicians present emotional conclusions as truth. This approach is being encouraged by those who want to profit from it.

In this book, I will explore how and why the American Coma has developed, continues to grow, and the danger this trend presents to our country. I will also offer actions we can take to reestablish a balance of emotional and rational thinking to deal with the challenges that face us all.

I am an ordinary citizen: a wife, mother, and teacher. I live the normal, busy life of most Americans. I grew up in the 1950's and went off to College in the 1960's.

I have been part of the trend I see in America today. I have lived by my emotions and left my rational brain asleep in the back seat. Now that I am waking up, I see the dangers of emotional thinking. To make good decisions, we need to wake up our rational brain and use a balanced approach to life.

We can greatly improve the direction of our lives, our country, and the world by spending just a little time seeking out more information before we make up our minds. What have other people done? What are politicians, scientists, other citizens, and the opposition saying or not saying? Do they offer background information or evidence for their position? What are the sources for the "facts" they present?

If we ask more questions, demand better answers, consider long-term consequences, and listen to other points of view we will come up with better solutions.

We have it good in the United States, although it's hard to see that when we look at the news. This has lulled us to sleep. We have become an easy target for conmen, liars, and thieves, as well as enemies outside our country. Who do we believe?

Now, more than ever, staying asleep is dangerous. With the communication technology available today it is easy to fool millions of people in a very short period of time. It is easy to steal billions of dollars, strip away fundamental rights in the name of protection, and amass unthinkable amounts of power and control over citizens if we are not paying attention.

Developing our reasoning abilities will help us sort it out together. We will always have disagreements but balancing our emotional and rational minds will allow us to consider all sides of an issue and cooperate to find the best solution. It will help us spot the conmen faster, keep more of our own money, and have more say about the direction of our lives and our country.

We, as individuals and a country, are works in progress. There is always more to learn, challenges to meet, improvements to be made, and dangers to face. Ordinary citizens are the power that keeps our country strong. It will only survive if we stay involved and vigilant. It is time for the quiet, ordinary citizens to speak up. It is our duty and our privilege to be the guardians of democracy.

Chapter 1
Emotion Is Not Enough

What is the most important quality in a human being? If you asked me that question 20 years ago I would have responded, "A kind and generous heart". That phrase sums up my belief about our purpose on Earth: to help each other live positive and fulfilling lives.

Today, I still respond with the same answer. However, as the rational part of my brain started to wake up from its long slumber, I realized that more is needed to truly help people. We need the balance of emotional feelings to inspire and rational thought to accomplish. I have become concerned that there is a spreading acceptance of making decisions purely on an emotional basis to the point of ignoring conflicting facts and evidence.

A growing number of Americans are walking around suffering from the American Coma. Part of their brain is not fully functional. I know, because for 26 years I was afflicted by this deep sleep myself. The ability to use logic, gather and analyze facts, and consider other opinions to find workable solutions is unused, untrained, and sleeping. What remains awake is the emotional side of the brain, free to take charge of all decision making.

The effect is an adult who functions much like an adolescent (or sometimes even a two year old child). Opinions are formed at a very young age and locked in with an emotional protective barrier. Once locked in, it is very difficult to break through with logic or facts. The emotional mind will only allow input that supports the locked-in world view and feeds the craving for emotional validation.

This leaves the adult out of balance. The same mistakes are made over and over again. A twisted, circular form of reason is sometimes used to distort or outright lie to protect the emotional opinion. The sleepers talk only to other sleepers, reaffirming their preconceived ideas, renewing the emotional fervor, and going out into the world determined to spread the "truth" as they feel it.

When someone intrudes with an opposing opinion they are dismissed with name calling and baseless accusations. Any attempt at discussion is met with an emotional monologue that seeks to misdirect and distract. No response is allowed from the opposition before the next accusation is thrown and a full-blown tantrum is enacted.

Not all sleepers are this severe. People are suffering a range of symptoms. However, it is spreading and becoming deeply embedded in the fabric of our country.

I believe America is in great danger from this sleeping epidemic. It has invaded the highest positions of government. It is allowing bad decisions to cost us trillions of dollars. The very people who cause the problems have control over solving them. Panic over a non-existent crisis gets our attention while real problems are ignored.

Ultimately, society could fully embrace the "take care of us" mentality that is being encouraged. Individuals will give up freedom, control, independence, and most of their money so government will take full responsibility for their well-being. As we sleep, others will continue to take advantage of us.

After my college "awakening" in the 1960's, I spent 26 years happily asleep. I voted for people who "cared". I gave little thought to planning my financial future or developing a career. I had little interest or trust in history, business, science, economics or my parent's opinions. I believed the poor were innocent victims and the rich were selfish villains. Small countries were noble and big powerful countries, (like the United States), were imposing bullies.

I believed that society needed to be reinvented. I reacted to conservative views with distain, immediately dismissing them as coming from uncaring, greedy people. I supported the Democrat Party politics blindly and fully believed, without question, that the liberal agenda would help people in need. I acted out of a desire to make the world a better place. This was a powerful motivation.

The Civil Rights Movement and the Viet Nam War were powerful, emotional events. Many of us thought we were going to change the world. We were hindered by ignorance and a lack of rational thought.

A great deal of change was, indeed, accomplished. Social awareness was increased, differences in people more widely accepted and a world of peace and prosperity for everyone seemed attainable.

However, even with noble intentions, operating with only an emotional brain and not following up with rational thought, can cause damage and limit changes. The very people we want to help remain in poverty, remain addicted to drugs, and continue to commit crimes. Social programs generate millions of dollars that never reach the people who need them. People often resent our interference. They see our desire to help as imposing our will uninvited, (often they are right), with little understanding of what is needed.

Sometimes the help is smothering, making people totally dependent on others rather than gaining the skills to become independent. Solutions are often delayed while effort and money are wasted. We feel good because we think we're doing something to help but we need to use the rational side of our brain to effectively solve problems.

There is another side to the emotional brain, a negative side. The emotional brain encourages self-indulgence and radical actions. Everything is acceptable and can be justified. Without the "brakes" of rational thought, emotions run the show. The end justifies the means. If it feels good, do it. What's in it for me? Other people are responsible for ruining my life.

People can become totally self-involved with no consideration for others. These people often turn to crime and violence to get what they want or to vent their anger. Their actions are often excused by other sleeping brains as justified because of abusive childhoods, denied opportunities, etc. Criminals are often seen as victims. They do a great deal of harm to themselves and others.

Misdirected help and self-indulgence create many problems but the sleeping brain allows a greater danger. The danger is from people who see this lack of rational thought as a true opportunity to manipulate the emotional "do-gooders" and the angry disenfranchised for their own selfish goals. For the people with sleeping brains are easy to fool.

Advertisers run emotional ads to sell their products. Cars are sold with pretty girls or promises of powerful, fast-accelerating engines that are of no use on real streets. For years, a bank ran television ads that did not promote a single service, competitive rate, or advantage to using their bank. The entire ad created an emotional tie between the bank and American dreams. The campaign was very successful.

To gain money, power, and control some have learned how to appeal to the emotional brain and get millions of people to follow blindly. No need for facts, scientific evidence, or common sense. All they need is a cause (real or not) that appeals to the "right a wrong" or "they owe me" feelings of a sleeping brain. Then, they create a fall guy to blame for the problem and they're ready to go. They loudly make an accusation and people will give them money, do their bidding, and put them in charge of solving the problem (which often they have caused or invented in the first place).

They never have to bother proving their accusation. Presenting evidence is unnecessary as long as they convince people that they are one of them. They are one of the caring, feeling, and save the world people. They are angry, too, about the unfair world that has cheated people of what they deserve. While these people are being hailed as heroes and earning millions of dollars, behind the scenes they are exacting terrible damage to individuals, our country, and our planet.

There have always been unscrupulous people. History is full of people who have taken advantage of others for their own selfish desires. The growing trend toward emotional thinking is making it easier for them to succeed.

P.T. Barnum would be proud. They are fooling many people most of the time. They are using the unchecked emotions of millions of people. They take our money, restrict our choices, limit news information, gain more control over our lives, and make us totally dependent. The sleeping people smile and say, "thank you". Sounds like a bad movie, doesn't it? The aliens are turning us into pod people.

There is hope for the future. It is possible to wake up the reasoning part of our brains and regain balance in our thinking. Balance is the key to everything in life. Feelings aren't bad they just need to be balanced with logical thinking. Freedom is balanced with responsibility. The rewards of life are balanced with the hard work. We must dream but be practical to achieve those dreams.

We need to re-educate ourselves by questioning, demanding evidence, and really listening to what people are saying. Do we have to spend hours a day researching issues? Most of us don't have the time. But if we pay just a little more attention to the news, listen to a few more sources, and think about what is said it could make a tremendous difference.

Chapter 2
Waking Up From a Long Sleep

In the mid 1990's something happened to me. I suddenly realized that, politically, I had turned into a conservative! My thoughts about most issues were more closely aligned with the Republican Party, not the Democratic Party! This was a bit of a shock to me and to this day is a complete mystery to some of my friends and family. What happened?

What happened was not an overnight revelation. No bolt of lightning hit me. It was a gradual change. I started listening carefully to what people were saying. I began to think about what they were saying. To my surprise, I didn't always agree with the Democrats I had followed for so many years. In fact, I rarely agreed with them.

I started listening to people on conservative talk radio while driving in the car. I was surprised by the way they talked about issues. They gave their opinion, explained their reasoning, and cited sources of information, usually in a calm manner. I was struck by the attitude of respect for their audience. They gave background information and encouraged their audience to seek out more information and make up their own minds. Just a few minutes of listening would give me so much to think about.

Yes, some of them use a bit of showmanship, humor and sometimes a bit of insulting sarcasm, which I personally don't care for. After listening for awhile, though, I found most of their discussions were respectful of people and focused on issues.

I want to thank people like Rush Limbaugh, Sean Hannity, Bill O'Reilly, Mark Levin, Rabbi Daniel Lapin, Dr. Bill Wattenburg, Brian Sussman, Barbara Simpson, and more for continuing to fight the good fight for balanced coverage of the news, informed analysis, and historical perspective.

I want to thank my husband, who has always asked questions and made me think about issues in different ways. His kind and generous heart won my heart and his curious mind keeps me thinking and growing.

I want to thank my parents. They planted the seeds of common sense and reason. They carefully taught respect for others, the rewards of hard work and the importance of living an honorable life. Even in the heady days of college indulgence, their voices of reason and common sense prevailed at many moments of decision. The seeds of reason these people planted in my brain have helped me wake up.

I was waking from a 26 year coma. Questions began to push their way into my groggy brain. I began to look at current issues in the news with a different perspective. I wanted more information.

War in Iraq: When a friend declared that the only reason we were meddling in Iraq was our interest in oil, I reacted with questions instead of my usual affirmation. Well, shouldn't our government look out for our interests? Are we wrong trying to stabilize an oil-producing country?

If you don't want our foreign policy to be influenced by the need for oil, shouldn't we be drilling for the vast reserves we have in our own country? I digress into a separate issue here but often issues are interconnected. Finding sensible solutions often requires us to connect the dots between issues. I talk about energy later in the chapter.

People have insisted that the war in Iraq had nothing to do with terrorists. Yet many terrorists from other countries came to disrupt the progress in Iraq. It seemed very important to terrorist groups. Maybe that indicated the outcome of Iraq was important to us, too.

Shouldn't we help a population who has been suffering under a tyrannical ruler for 30 years? Saddam Hussein gave every indication of being very aggressive and cruel with no regard for human rights. He attacked a sovereign country, Kuwait. He used biological weapons on his own citizens.

People still declare we were lied to by President Bush and there were no weapons of mass destruction

(I think biological weapons qualify). Yet, I heard military reports of many discoveries of biological weapons, evidence of weapons factories, and citizens of Iraq testifying to massive operations to hide weapons. After all, Hussein had years to cover up and move things while we waited in vain for the United Nations to enforce resolutions. I still wonder what is hiding in Syria and the deserts of Iraq.

There were reports that all the countries around Iraq were very worried about Hussein, who was considered a "loose cannon". He had demonstrated his willingness to sacrifice his own people to carry out his threats. He wasn't just talk. All of this was ignored by most media. Why?

Reports from soldiers in Iraq talked about the enormous progress in rebuilding roads and schools. They were training Iraqi soldiers, police, and government officials. They talked about the enormous outpouring of thankfulness from the Iraqi people. Millions of Iraqi citizens risked their lives to vote in their first elections.

Why was so much of this information only reported by a few news agencies and talk shows? Why was so much information hidden from the American public? Who benefited from the misperception of failure in Iraq?

Then President-elect, Obama, announced a new plan for Iraq. As soon as he took office, he would be moving toward a responsible withdrawal from Iraq while training the Iraqi people to run their own country. Had he been asleep? Perhaps he hoped we had. We had been working toward this goal all along. He had not re-invented the wheel.

Are the Iraqi people better off now? I believe they are. They have a chance to create a new government. They have a say in their future. They have hope, but the future will not be easy for them.

No major change comes without pain and sacrifice for all involved. When a power vacuum is created, groups seeking power come out of the woodwork. It takes time for order to be restored, for a new government to get organized, especially when opposing forces are trying to stop any progress. Perhaps, we Americans need to develop some patience and long-term thinking.

The **war in Afghanistan** has also cost many lives and a great deal of money. We accepted our action there because there was a clear connection to the 911 attack in New York. Yet, it is hard to continue being involved over many years. We should constantly re-evaluate, look for other ways to accomplish our goals, and clearly define the threats that face us.

Islamic terrorism: We cannot ignore the real danger of radical Islamic groups. These are violent groups with a desire for world power. They have hidden under a blanket of religion to use and sacrifice their followers. Since the 1970's, there has been a rapidly growing movement within the Muslim world.

The leaders of these groups have been brainwashing thousands of children in schools that require them to chant mindlessly, "Death to America!", and "America, the great Satan". These leaders have kept their people in poverty and despair while convincing them that outsiders are to blame. They have built a revolutionary army.

We cannot underestimate the danger. We cannot ignore the threat and hope the danger will go away. For the past forty years, we have continued to let violent attacks go largely unanswered. 911 woke us up to the danger but it is hard to stay alert and aware over a long period of time. The terrorists count on our inattention.

We have to face the facts. These groups are ruthless, violent, clever and patient. They have declared war on the free world and will use every method available to destroy us. They use intimidation, brainwashing, and violence to keep their followers in line. I just heard about a 14 year old girl in Afghanistan who was shot in the head because she thought girls should be educated. (Thankfully, she survived.) They have no problem murdering their own people. They will not hesitate to kill Westerners when given a chance.

These groups are active in countries all over the world. They continue to grow. Talking to them, apologizing to them, appeasing them, and giving in to their demands will not stop them. While we pass resolutions, they use the time to become stronger. They act boldly when we back down.

War has been declared. It was declared many years ago. Violent acts continue against us. The latest round of attacks on our embassies resulted in the murder of four Americans, including our ambassador, in Libya.

We must be active in this fight. Passive responses will only embolden our enemy. Make no mistake. These terrorists will fight to the death. Their followers believe they are joining a holy war. They will not stop until we force them to stop. Yet, our government downplays the danger, tries to give us the impression that with the death of Bin Laden we no longer have to worry. Why do the administration and the mainstream media continue to keep important information away from the American People?

I do not take lightly the loss of American lives, the sacrifices our military families are making and the financial cost. Is it worth the cost? We need facts, calm discussion, and experts in military strategy, foreign relations, history, and economics, etc. working together to make sensible decisions.

I'm afraid all the name calling and emotional rabble-rousing from many politicians will not help us decide on the best course of action. It is done only to promote themselves and their own party. People who act this way should not be re-elected.

We need to train our brains to separate the meaningless noise from useful information and sincere contribution from selfish actions.

The Economy: For years I have heard politicians blame big business for economic woes. Big oil is greedy. Banks are gouging their mortgage customers. A crisis would make headlines and Congress would immediately call the CEO's of these companies to appear before a congressional committee. They would be interrogated for endless hours about their culpability in the current problem.

For years I accepted as fact that big business was greedy and evil. They needed to be regulated, watched, and punished whenever possible. Then, I began to think about it. Why were the rich considered bad guys? Weren't they the ones who invested in our economy? Weren't they the people who were smart, successful, and took the risk to make businesses work and grow? Didn't they create the jobs our economy needed? Weren't growing profits a good thing?

I began to listen to talk radio programs and Fox news. The hosts had guest experts from many different fields, including economics. They explained how lowering taxes and encouraging investment helps our economy grow and how raising taxes and adding invasive regulations can hurt our economy. I began to learn how our economy works. It made sense.

A free market economy works when business growth is encouraged. When government gets out of the way, citizens work hard, invent, invest, and get rewarded. The economy grows and everybody benefits. More jobs are created, a better standard of living is achieved, more taxes are collected without raising rates, and more disposable income is available to help those in need. History has shown that this approach works. It does not make government more powerful. Some see this as a problem.

If a company or individual breaks the law, they should be prosecuted. We have laws to do this. Entire companies or industries should not be vilified for the actions of a few individuals.

When politicians point fingers of blame we need to look deeper than the simple explanations they give us. Why have politicians been misleading us all these years? The misdeeds of a few CEO's, although serious, have caused economic problems that are very small compared to the harm the government has done to our economy.

For example, Congress imposed laws and regulations designed to force banks to make high-risk loans. To get elected, politicians promised the American dream of owning your own home. They needed the appearance of providing the opportunity in order to get re-elected. Politicians wanted people who didn't qualify for loans to get them anyway. They wanted to get credit for making their voters happy.

I saw this happen first hand. I was a mortgage underwriter in the 1980's and 90's. The lenders knew it was not good business to make high-risk loans. Unfortunately, banks were forced to make loans to borrowers who could not afford them. This created disaster for the borrowers, the banks, and the economy of the country. This meltdown was caused by years of high-risk lending dictated by the Federal Government. Yet, the very people who caused this problem are rewarded and put in charge of solving the problem. Government still tries to point the finger of blame at greedy banks and businesses.

The free market economy is a win-win situation. It allows business, innovation, and job growth. It gives consumers more choice, better products, and better prices through competition. All that's needed to keep our economy running smoothly are a few basic laws to keep criminal activity in check and keep consumers informed.

The Environment and Energy: Protecting clean air, water, and soil seems like a slam-dunk goal. Who could object to it? We all want to live healthier lives and keep the Earth in good shape for our children, right? I followed and supported the environmental movement for many years. As I woke up from my coma, more nagging questions started percolating in my brain.

People were catching on that there was big money to be made in the environmental movement. Companies could be sued $$$$. The public would donate $$$$. Laws could be passed $$$$. Lies would be believed $$$$. Lawyers and politicians could make a very nice income.

Environmental boards are appointed and answer to no one. In California, incredible decisions have been made causing damage to many people and businesses and costing tax payers millions of dollars. They have demanded new formulations of gas to "reduce emissions from automobiles". They insisted on a reformulation of diesel fuel that ate through fuel lines. The reformulation of regular gas created higher costs and less efficient mileage so any reduction of emissions was cancelled out.

The people on these boards were given the position as a political reward. They are not established scientists in these fields and they do not seem to seek the advice of scientists. These new fuels were not tested sufficiently before being mandated for the entire state. Legislators are making these appointments and bragging to the public about how much they are doing to help the environment.

Another decision in California that cost millions and put many independent gas station owners out of business was the demand that all gas holding tanks be dug up and replaced. The fear was the possibility of gas leaking into the ground and polluting water sources.

Some scientists say there were easy, cost-effective ways to test for and correct any problems. If true, Scientists and engineers could have saved those business owners and the tax payers millions of dollars. Why weren't other solutions considered? Many independent station owners were put out of business. They just couldn't afford to dig up the tanks, pull out any contaminated soil and put in new tanks. Someone made a great deal of money from that decision and it is always the consumer who pays the price. It is up to the public to demand solutions that make sense, don't waste our tax money, and don't destroy businesses and property needlessly.

Environmental groups fomented a panic mentality about nuclear power. It was easy to convince emotional minds. They succeeded in stopping any further building of nuclear power plants with emotional scare tactics that contained few facts.

Some groups have no problem using lies to scare us. The "end justifies the means" thinking is a big part of emotionalism. Meanwhile, power plants were built in Europe and have served them well to produce inexpensive, safe energy.

I was on the bandwagon for many years. Then I started listening to other people, hearing some facts I had not heard before. (Thank you, Bill Wattenburg.) I started thinking and questioning. Yes, there have been some accidents. However, with precautions and new technology, nuclear plants can be very safe and nuclear waste safely stored.

There is no need to completely abandon this efficient form of energy. There are factors to be considered. It might be better to expand our nuclear energy output. How about the economic benefits of having cheaper energy?

We have vast reserves of oil within our own country, yet we are still depending on outside sources. Environmental groups are driving the anti-drilling movement with fear. It is a common method of gaining emotional followers. It is costing us untold billions by forcing us to buy from foreign countries what we already have. This dependence on foreign countries for our oil also affects our foreign policies and our country's security. It doesn't make sense to me.

Environmentalists insist we will hurt the environment by drilling for oil. Oil platforms may not look pretty as part of the ocean view, but they have been proven safe. (Since I wrote this, an oil rig exploded in the Gulf. There is always danger of accident or sabotage in any endeavor. I still feel that ocean drilling is very safe overall. Of course, if our government would allow drilling closer to shore it would be even safer.) The pipeline in Alaska has not destroyed the wilderness around it. The only damage has been from violent attacks by radical environmentalists. Now, they object to drilling in Alaska because it will hurt the environment and wildlife. There is no evidence of this. Past drilling projects do not support this claim.

Developing clean, non-polluting forms of energy is the path to the future. As we develop these new sources, we need a common sense attitude. These sources will not be available or efficient overnight.

Looking at the current status of clean energy sources, the cheapest way to produce electricity is nuclear and hydro-electric power. The most expensive, inefficient ways are solar and wind power. Why is our government subsidizing the most expensive methods?

Our economy (and, therefore, our energy needs) must grow or it will implode. A growing economy is what gives us the extra income to invest in research, fund inventors and help people in need. It occurs to me that if we use current fuels available to produce less expensive energy, we could use that saved money to speed up the research of future clean and renewable sources of energy. A win-win scenario!

Global Warming: I listened carefully to the alarmist warnings. The oceans would swallow the coastal areas. The ice caps were melting at a dangerous rate. Man is heating up the Earth with pollution. We need to lower our carbon footprint, stop using fossil fuels, and develop clean energy as soon as possible. (But don't use nuclear energy, don't build new energy plants.) This is a world-wide crisis. We must all act now!!! Al Gore will save us. Send in your money, Nobel honors and don't forget to buy the book and movie.

Wait a minute! Exactly what evidence do we have that humans are affecting the temperature of the Earth? The glaciers are receding! Yes, one or two glaciers are receding. Yet most are growing at this point say scientists who have physical evidence to back up their claim. Hmm, that doesn't fit the crisis. Very few news outlets have even mentioned the growing glaciers. Why?

Polar bears are endangered! We're destroying their habitat! There is a much larger population of polar bears today than in the 1950's. (Yes, there are people who go out and count polar bears. It's called gathering scientific facts.) Again, claims don't exactly fit the facts. Perhaps we need more information.

Global warming proponents claim that overall temperatures around the Earth have been increasing. Yes, they appeared to be for a few years, but in the last 16 years they have not been increasing. Hmm, that doesn't fit. There are serious questions about how and where temperature measurements were made and how they were compared to earlier measurements. Why haven't news outlets been talking about all the information available?

The phrase, "a consensus of scientists agree that global warming is happening", is interesting. Notice how carefully this is worded. A consensus means more that one. They never say a majority. I find that curious. It's a fine example of a statement that sounds very impressive but means nothing.

What evidence do these scientists offer to back up their claim? They have made computer models to project into the future. A computer model will only project the future based on the information that people have input. Can we really believe all factors involved in the climate system of the Earth have been considered in these computer models? Do these computer models really take into account the climate patterns of hundreds of thousands of years? To back up their claims they offer a few carefully chosen events around the Earth. These events do not represent studied patterns but rather individual events that appear to support the preconceived conclusion. This is science at its worse. They ignore good scientific research and methods.

The man-made global warming theory is presented as irrefutable scientific fact for one reason. That's where the opportunity is for making money and taking control. Now that evidence shows the Earth is not currently warming, a new catch phrase is being used. "Climate Change" is the new danger. It is another impressive sounding but meaningless phrase. The climate is always changing. Change cannot be disproved and for the emotional, "humans are evil" crowd that is enough to prove man is the cause.

Scientists that have spent over 30 years studying climate changes and patterns have come to vastly different conclusions about our current climate and temperature status. S. Fred Singer and Dennis T. Avery have written a book called "Unstoppable Global Warming", Rowman and Littlefield Publishers, Inc. 2007.

They offer 30 years of research and millions of years of physical evidence to explain the cycles of climate changes on the Earth. They offer information that you never hear on the news. The Earth has incredible systems in place that restore the balance of temperature and climate.

Patterns seen in cores drilled all over the Earth show what we are experiencing is a normal pattern that has repeated over and over across millions of years. There are patterns within patterns, enormous forces at work, including sun activity. Yet, many are insisting mankind is causing or, at least, accelerating climate changes. Why?

We keep hearing about the danger of increasing CO_2 in the atmosphere. It is presented as a poison, as a cause of global warming. In fact, it is an essential, but very small, part of our atmosphere that has a natural pattern of increase and decrease. Elevated amounts actually increase plant productivity. When CO_2 gets too high, the Earth has the ability to adjust. This is supported by physical and historical evidence.

Perhaps, we should be considering the possibility that we need to adjust to climate changes. If we can't control the climate then we need to find ways to cope with variations in precipitation, temperature, etc. We can find ways to be flexible with agriculture, food, water, and population distribution.

Why do media organizations ignore scientific information? Who gains by keeping us uninformed about these issues? To make good decisions, we need all the information available and we should insist on it.

It bothers me that the fear-mongers shouting about global warming are taking our attention and available money away from real problems. There are real environmental problems that need our informed attention.

We have made great strides in the United States over the past 40 years. Air pollution, water pollution, over-logging, and over-fishing are just some of the problems that have been greatly improved.

I agree that there are environmental issues that are global. We need to help other countries improve the levels of pollution they are producing. Countries like China, who are charging ahead with old technologies, are creating vast amounts of pollution that directly affect our air. We need to be very careful and find solutions that are efficient, effective and based on good scientific and economic principles.

Getting additional information has changed my thinking on these issues. It isn't easy to find sources that will offer a different point of view. Seeing the growing success of conservative talk radio and Fox News indicates that more citizens are seeking additional information. They, too, are not satisfied with the emotional approach. It gives me hope that reason will become a balanced part of solving problems.

Chapter 3
Where Did It Start?

Post-war America was in full recovery mode in the 1950's. After the hardship of the Depression and World War II, Americans were hard at work pursuing the peacetime American Dream. The middle class was booming. Businesses were started. Men were glad to work hard at a job, marry the girl next door and start raising a family. One working parent could support a family, buy a home and carefully save for retirement.

After experiencing the Depression and World War II, parents knew that hard work, careful saving and planning for the future was necessary to achieve some sense of security. Many of their children did not experience the same life lessons.

A life of ease often brings out a sense of entitlement. We expected to have plenty to eat, a home, a good education. The luxuries of more free time and spare money allowed for the indulgence of looking beyond our own day-to-day existence. As we went off to college, or out into the workforce, we became aware that life isn't always perfect for other people. It was an emotional awakening.

I went off to college in the 1960's. I protested the Viet Nam War and thought only my generation had kind and generous hearts. I wanted to change the world. Anyone who disagreed with me just didn't get it or didn't care about people the way I did. Sound familiar?

At this stage, the emotional awakening resulted in a distrust of government, the establishment, and the previous generation. This presented a unique challenge to politicians. I believe this distrust was the catalyst for the intensive us against them mentality that exists today between the Democrat and Republican Parties.

A politician had to convince the young voters of the 60's that he/she was of the new vanguard leading the charge to throw out business-as-usual in Washington, D.C. (and state capitals across the nation). To be re-elected, politicians had to turn on each other. Cooperation and compromise were done behind closed doors.

Rapidly over the last 50 years name calling and blaming have increasingly become the order of the day, especially for the Democratic Party. The Democrats pinned their hopes for their political future on the young and the poor. They became experts at appealing to the emotional mind. This approach isn't embraced only by Democrats but it appears to have become officially engrained as part of the Democratic Party mindset. The Democrats have been moving toward radical, liberal causes for many years. This approach has become so successful that many people still believe government is evil and at the same time that government will solve all their problems. Only the emotional mind can handle the illogic.

As we embraced the emotional awakening, both positive and negative emotional attitudes were growing. The emotions of social justice were getting stronger but so were the emotions of arrogance and self-indulgence.

The 1960's started a movement that continues to grow today. This movement has changed our society immensely. The, "Make love, not war. If it feels right, do it.", crowd has grown up. We have become parents, teachers, writers, lawyers, judges, reporters, and politicians.

For some, the zeal to reinvent a society full of love, understanding, and acceptance has turned into an arrogant, "I know more than you. Agree with me or leave", attitude. They have become as close-minded as the "establishment" they protested in the 1960's.

It is human nature to protect what you have. As the "flower children" of the sixties grew older and more prosperous, those who emerged as leaders began to protect their own status quo and consolidate their own power and influence.

The result is what we see today, leaders who use a veneer of positive emotional attitudes, "We must help the minorities, the poor, etc." to promote their own negative, protective attitudes, "I am entitled to be rich, powerful, and in charge. I know what is best for you."

As we were raising our emotional awareness, we were rejecting reason and common sense. The human body lives by the "use it or lose it" rule. If we don't use the reasoning part of our brain, it goes to sleep.

As young adults began to have children, they taught them to tune in to their emotions. They neglected to teach them how to use linear thought, reason through a problem, consider many sides of a question to find the best solution, and control their emotions.

These skills need to be taught and practiced to reach proficiency. Obviously, if people haven't perfected these skills in themselves, they can't teach them to others. So over the past 50 years, the emotional mind epidemic has spread and is carried through the generations.

◁▷

Chapter 4
Emotionalism Keeps Spreading

How has this deep sleep of the rational mind spread so widely through our society? For people to continue with this emotional approach there must be some benefit or, at least, a perceived benefit. What makes us content to stay in this emotional state?

There are lies in this emotional life that are comforting to believe. I am not responsible for the problems in my life. There is no use trying, outside forces will prevent me from succeeding. If I fail, government will take care of me. If rational thinking is not part of the equation it is easy to believe the comforting lies.

Why is it so appealing? If we believe that outside forces have caused our problems we absolve ourselves from any responsibility to work toward fixing the problems. Self-examination is hard. Admitting we may play some part in causing our problems means we need to take some action, make changes, and work at improving our lives. For many of us, it is easier to continue dealing with personal relationships, work, and financial problems in the same way we have in the past.

Searching for a life partner becomes a series of negative experiences with losers, users, and abusers. Looking for the great paying job becomes a series of interviews for jobs we are not qualified for, taking jobs we can't handle with disagreeable co-workers or bosses, and constant layoffs in a field with a history of no security.

We spend our lives hoping that outside forces will change and that continuing to approach our life in the same way, over and over again, will somehow give us a different result. Is this rational? No, it is an emotional approach to life that is doomed to failure or, at least, no improvement.

Why are people content with this approach? The benefit is the emotional comfort that we are not to blame. The failures are not our responsibility. We can blame our troubles on luck, the economy, or the political party in power. We can feel sorry for ourselves, get others to feel sympathy for us, and depend on others to help us. We believe outside forces control our lives, cause our problems, and can fix our problems. We become susceptible to empty promises.

If we believe that others will prevent us from succeeding then we don't have to put out any effort at all. Why try when we know we will fail? It isn't our fault. Others have made it impossible for us to achieve our goals. If we give up before we start there is no risk of failure. It is easier to blame others and continue along the same path. It takes very little effort to complain, whine, and accuse.

If we are convinced that others have prevented us from achieving success then we also believe that others owe us. We want others to make it up to us. We want to be protected in our job even if we aren't doing it very well. We want the best health care, the best schools, and a secure retirement even if we can't pay anything for it. "It's our right! They owe it to us!" People can accept total dependence or turn to crime and violence then justify it with a, "The world owes me.", attitude.

This is where the emotional "blame others" attitude really pays off. The "I am entitled" belief has been changing our country dramatically. It has given birth to a wide array of social government programs. It has created an expectation that everyone is entitled to everything. The idea that we have to work hard and work smart to earn things in life has been forgotten. This kind of thinking leads to fewer and fewer productive citizens carrying the burden for more and more unproductive citizens.

Reason and logic will tell us that this kind of behavior will only lead to disaster for any civilization. At some point, the productive part of the society becomes overloaded and can no longer support the unproductive sector.

Yet, some people encourage this type of emotional thinking. Why? What do they have to gain from encouraging the dependent expectations? If someone is ambitious for money, power, and control it is the perfect opportunity. They can create an illusion and appeal to the emotions of the dependent. They can easily convince us to hand over our money, put people in positions of power, and abdicate control of our lives.

Advertising, politics, business, charities are just a few of the areas that offer endless opportunities to take advantage of the emotional dependent. It is big business. The stakes keep getting higher and the scam artists are getting bolder and more dangerous by the minute. Billions and billions of dollars are wasted and outright stolen. The money makes the scam artists rich and it is no longer available to those who earned it or to those in need.

We must accept the responsibility and take charge of our own lives. Our first reaction to any problem should be, "What can I do to improve the situation?" We can change our attitudes and play an active role in determining the direction of our future. Freedom is possible only by accepting responsibility. Every day we make choices. These choices are what chart the direction of our lives. Outside forces can affect us but only as much as we allow.

Tragedies occur. People lose family, possessions, and jobs. Some have been abused, some are disabled. The list goes on but we are still in charge of our lives. We choose how to react and what to do next.

Choice is an essential freedom. To make good choices we need the balance of the rational and emotional brain. We need to carefully consider our options, what we want to achieve and the steps necessary to reach our goal. Our goal may be to make more money, spend more time with our family, or find a job that is personally fulfilling. The goals of individuals are varied. The goals of our country must encourage our freedom of choice and our individual responsibility.

Let's ask questions and demand reasonable answers. We should assess problems not just for immediate relief but long-term solutions. What will be the results of our actions? Every action has a ripple effect. We need to carefully analyze the next effect and the next, etc.

As a society, we should seek input from experts in science, economics, history, and international relations, not just from politicians and their appointees. This country is full of millions of people who have experience, creative ideas, and have proven their ability to live responsible, problem-solving lives. We must demand in-depth answers, not the glib, bumper sticker language we are getting from our leaders. Let's start sharing our ideas. To create a balance of emotional and rational thinking we need to help each other. We need to listen, talk, question, and discuss.

Chapter 5
Government Is Not Good Business

Remember the phrase, "cut out the middle man"? We all look for bargains where we can go directly to the manufacturer or wholesale distributor to get a better price. Consumers understand. The distributors, salesmen, and stores all have costs and need to make a profit. The more layers, the more cost. The cost is always passed on to the consumer.

Accountability becomes another problem. More layers make it harder to trace a problem to its source. The responsible party becomes further removed from the consumer. Poor quality, inefficiency, shortages, and theft become easier to hide. Blame can be shifted from one department to another with no satisfaction for the consumer.

Competition is a consumer's power in a free market economy. When companies must compete for our business they are motivated to improve their product or service and lower prices. The consumer wins.

When there is no competition, there is no motivation to improve products and lower prices. The consumer's wishes are no longer important. We can't take our business elsewhere.

The same principles apply to government. The more layers involved, the more cost to the American Public. The larger a bureaucracy becomes the more difficult the accountability. Government run industries and programs eliminate competition. The consumer's needs and desires are no longer a major part of the equation. The individual is far removed from any consideration when decisions are made.

Being re-elected causes some concern. However, officials only have to convince the voters they're doing a good job. They can easily hide what is going on in a large bureaucracy, shift blame to others and make voters feel that the official is fighting for the public good.

Government subsidized health care, stimulus packages, and bailouts of banks and auto manufacturers are not free. It is paid for by us, the citizens who pay more taxes. We not only give more of our money to government officials, we also give them our trust to spend it wisely.

Sadly, I do not trust government to do these tasks to benefit our economy or citizens. The federal government has a long history of designing programs in haste and then running them into the ground. Inefficiency, waste, fraud and damaging consequences for the public are often the results.

Some programs are deliberately designed to take more money and more control from the public. Government officials may believe they are taking control for the "public good" but we must be careful about what control we give to government. In the name of protection, we must always give up some of our freedom. Is it an acceptable trade?

Dealing with government is often a very frustrating experience. Trying to get an answer from the Department of Motor Vehicles, Social Security Administration, Internal Revenue Service, or Medicare can be difficult and confusing.

Beyond frustration, these entities are badly managed. Funds are taken to be used for other government functions and never paid back, waste and fraud are constant problems and the possibility of bankruptcy is often in the news.

Waste and misuse of public funds is not new. However, the scale of spending and the brazen way it is now occurring is unprecedented. From 2008 to 2010, when the Democrats were in charge of both houses of Congress as well as the Presidency, the federal government passed bill after bill to spend trillions of our dollars for vague programs. They literally wrote trillions of dollars in blank checks to President Obama's administration to spend any way they wanted. The willingness of Congress to allow the President to have such control is very dangerous and seriously threatens the balance of power and the checks and balances that are wisely built into the Constitution.

When government grows over time we may not notice how invasive it becomes in our lives. It has been growing at an ever increasing rate and we have reached a tipping point. Some of our leaders have become completely consumed with power for themselves and consolidating power for their party.

Healthcare:

To illustrate how out of control our leaders have become, let's take a look at what happened with the Obama healthcare bill (now law). While the Democrats held the White House and control of Congress, there was a push to get a healthcare bill passed before the mid-term elections. Speaker of the House Nancy Pelosi, Senator Harry Reid, and President Obama were leading the push to get their healthcare bill passed into law. The bill kept growing and despite Republican protests that more time was needed to read and understand the now 2,800 page bill, it was pushed through the House and Senate and passed.

The incredible part of this vote was that Congress passed a bill they had not read! The Democratic leadership had such total control of Congress that they could convince them to vote for it. When Nancy Pelosi was asked what was in the bill, she replied, "You have to pass the bill to find out what is in it." What?!!! Why was it so important to keep the contents of this bill hidden? This is not the behavior of responsible lawmakers. This is the behavior of elected officials who, along with the President's administration are making a huge power play before people can find out what they are doing.

Since the bill became law, many have studied what is actually contained in the bill. The few sections I have read and heard about worry me a great deal.

A commission will be appointed (not elected by the people). They will decide what level of insurance coverage is required for every American. The law has amendments to the Internal Revenue Code and Social Security Act that allow the IRS to become the enforcer for the Health Commissioner and eliminate limits on gathering private information about any citizen regarding medical and financial records.

The penalties for not having this level of coverage will be imposed by the IRS. (They have already hired 3,000 new employees.) The penalties appear to be designed to encourage employers and individuals to choose the government option as private insurance plans become too expensive.

President Obama stated very clearly in speeches before he ran for President that his goal was nationalized healthcare. He said it may have to be done in steps. This law provides the power for the federal government to take those steps and completely take over one-sixth of our private business economy.

A phrase that is repeated numerous times throughout the law is, "to be determined by the Secretary of the Department of Health and Human Services." This leaves the law wide open to the whims of one person who is appointed by the President. So it appears that one-sixth of the economy has been nationalized and is controlled by the president and his appointee.

Once this program is fully implemented, the primary concern of government employees will be to keep it running, to cut costs, ration care and increase taxes to pay for it. The opinion of the doctor for the best care of the patient will not be a priority. If you are not satisfied, there will be no choices available, no appeal allowed, and no competition to provide an incentive for improvement of services.

Healthcare is an important issue. It requires careful research, discussion, and consideration. Trying solutions at local or state levels allow many programs to be tried. It allows tailoring of programs to fit the local situations. Medical personnel and local officials who are closer to the people involved will come up with better solutions. It is easier for the public to monitor the effectiveness and costs of local programs, keeping more control where it belongs, in the hands of our citizens.

Utah is trying reforms that allow employees to have access to a wide range of choices from private health insurance companies through a central streamlined clearinghouse. This makes it easier for employers to leave the choices open to their employees rather than lock into one or two programs that eliminate competition. I want to let reforms like this have a chance at state levels. It lets all of us see how different plans work or don't work.

I recently heard a news story about a woman in Oregon. Oregon has a required state health insurance program. This woman was having another bout of cancer after being in remission. Her doctor recommended an aggressive chemo therapy treatment. A government insurance bureaucrat denied approval of the treatment. He did offer to cover hospice care and/or assisted suicide! His stated reason, "treatment is not cost effective". Do you want to pay taxes all your working life for this kind of coverage? I don't. Perhaps, citizens of Oregon can move to Utah for a better chance of survival.

The universal health care idea fits into the pattern of, "We need to take care of everyone.", "They owe me.", and "It's not my fault.", emotional thinking. Politicians have been only too happy to encourage this expectation. It gives them an opportunity to tout government medical insurance programs that will "cover everybody". They shout, "You are denying citizens their "right" to health care" if you oppose these programs.

No government program is free. Universal health care will have a huge cost. You may think it's free when you don't pay at the doctor's office. In fact, you have pre-paid with your taxes. Just like every other government program, the additional layers of middlemen will add to the cost. Taxes will go higher, productivity will drop, efficiency, and accuracy will plummet.

Do we want clinics and hospitals that are staffed by overworked and underpaid people? What will happen to the incentives to become a doctor or do medical research?

We should look at nationalized healthcare programs in other countries. They provide a living example of how healthcare can become impersonal and inefficient. People often complain when dealing with their current insurance companies. It is reasonable to forecast that a health plan run by the federal government to cover over 300 million people will add thousands and thousands of additional government employees and only increase these problems.

Competition and the free market give the consumer the power of choice. I believe keeping healthcare services as private businesses and letting competition increase will provide better service and lower costs. Less government interference will allow citizens to have the final say about their own health.

A safety net for those unable to afford healthcare should be handled on a local level where care can be tailored to the needs of the individual and accountability will be much easier to maintain.

Social Security: Should government be in charge of your retirement money? Social Security funds have been collected by the government since the 1930's. The idea was to set aside this money, invest it, and give it back to us when we retired. That is the way it was sold to the public. It is not a savings plan but rather another way to tax the public. When the constitutionality of Social Security was challenged, Roosevelt won the decision by presenting it to the Supreme Court as a tax, not a forced savings! (Sound familiar? The Supreme Court recently declared the Health Care Law constitutional because it is a tax.) We have no say in how the money is invested and no say in how much we can get back. It's our own hard-earned money! The government is allowed to "borrow" this money and use it to pay for other government programs. Is there anyone who thinks they couldn't do a better job of caring for their retirement money than the government? This is another example of the inefficiency, waste and fraud inherent in government. Government officials convince us that we need to be "taken care of" and "protected". It is a means of taking control over more of our money. The underlying message is that we, the citizens, are not smart enough to run our own lives.

Government takeover of Private Business: Recently, the Federal Government stepped in to attempt "saving" some private businesses. They offered bailout money for financial institutions and auto manufacturers. This has been done before. Remember the airline industry? This time, however, the government demanded an "ownership" share of some private businesses and President Obama and his administration started telling these businesses how to run the business, who to fire and how much employees are allowed to earn. President Obama appointed a "pay czar" to determine what salaries and bonuses are allowed for executives of companies involved in the bailouts. This pay czar was not elected. He answered to no one but the President. One man was allowed to decide what employees of private companies should be paid. There were no guidelines by Congress, no recourse for the employees involved. There was no respect for lawful contracts agreed to by employer and employee. This does not sound like the democratic, free-market republic our founders set up.

Private businesses should be allowed to succeed or fail based on the management by company employees and the power of the consumer. Why should our tax dollars be used to pour billions into firms like Solyndra, a company that was obviously not going to be able to compete with the global market? Time and time again, we see examples of government officials who don't seem to have any common sense, let alone any good business sense when they are spending our hard-earned money. Perhaps, they have a different agenda for sending billions of taxpayer dollars to certain people and companies. Somehow, I don't believe it is for the common good.

Taxes: Taxes are collected to run government. The cleverness at getting more money from citizens is amazing. The withholding system has kept people unaware of the huge tax bill they pay. By taking a little out of each pay check, we quickly get used to the "net" figure on our paycheck and barely glance at the small amount that is taken out. How loudly would we scream for tax relief if we all had to write one huge check in April for our yearly tax bill? Don't forget about the taxes on what we buy, gift, transfer, inherit, etc. Let's also add in the registration fees, licensing fees that are required for automobiles, fishing, and pets. We pay use fees and sales tax for parks, bridge crossing, cable TV, telephones, gasoline, food, furniture, etc.

Taxes are not only used to pay for necessary government functions, they are also used to control the behavior of citizens. The idea that the government can control the public's behavior by hitting them in the wallet has taken hold big time. Taxes are used to punish unwanted behavior and windfall rewards are used to encourage wanted behavior. Those few in power decide what behavior is wanted or unwanted. Smokers must pay very high taxes on cigarettes. Drivers of cars must pay high taxes on gasoline. The "cash for clunkers" program in California has been used to reward people for buying a more fuel efficient car.

I have no argument with many of these goals. I am happy to see people stop smoking and buy fuel efficient cars. My objection is the methods used by government to interfere in our private lives and choices. Why does the tax code contain volumes of laws and regulations? The IRS is used to control aspects of our economy and our behavior. Layers and layers of new laws and regulations adjust our tax bill according to how we earn money, how we spend our money, how many children we have, what kind of energy we use to heat and cool our house, etc. The list is endless. How far are we willing to go with that approach? The average tax payer is losing 50% of their money to these taxes. That means we spend half of our working life paying the government. I think we're paying too much and getting very little in return. I would rather pay less for smaller government and make my own decisions on how my money should be spent, saved, and given away.

Hope springs eternal, at least for the emotional mind. People believe that more government will make their lives better. Rational minds, however, look at history and experience. Proposals need to be researched, discussed, and looked at from more than one perspective. The long-term effects of any change should be carefully considered. This takes time. The rush-it-through mentality of the current administration raises many red flags for me. I want to know why they don't want people to have enough time to even read a bill, let alone discuss it and get expert input before voting. What about giving the public enough time to have their say?

Government is cumbersome. It is a big, unmanageable organization. It does not strive to become efficient or provide good service. It does not have competition. It offers opportunities for waste, inefficiency and fraud. It creates such convoluted bureaucracy, laws and regulations that even the people administrating the programs aren't sure how it applies to individual situations. All of this costs more of our money and offers less benefit.

Government never produces income. It is the ultimate consumer. The business of government is to spend our money. The bigger government becomes, the more of our money it takes and the less say we have in how the money is spent.

Since government is not an income producing business trying to make a profit, it isn't run like a business. There is no incentive to keep down expenses. In fact, the opposite is true. Government agencies are rewarded for spending as much as they can. If a department saves money and runs efficiently, it will probably be punished by having its budget cut. If a department wastes money and spends its entire budget, it can apply for budget increases. More money equals more power and influence which creates bigger budgets, more money, and more power. All you need to do is spend the money and give the illusion of accomplishing something. Once a program or department has been established, it becomes an automatic item in the budget.

I have come to the conclusion that we should keep government, especially federal government, out of our lives as much as possible. The bulk of government functions should be kept at the state and local levels.

Federal government creates laws, regulations and programs with a "one size fits all" mentality. People, cities and states have different problems, situations and circumstances. Solutions need to be more flexible and more in tune with local needs.

Keeping more government functions at state and local levels also increases the ability of citizens to "keep an eye" on what's going on. It is easier to see results, what works and who works on a local level. The faster we can correct mistakes the better.

We need to go back to the basic principles of our founding fathers. Our Constitution was set up to give citizens the maximum freedom over their own lives without infringing on another citizen's freedom. The role of federal government was carefully spelled out.

The balance of power between the three branches of the federal government protects us from too much power in the hands of one individual or small group. The federal government is to play a very small role. Most of the functions of government are allocated to the state and local level.

We have gradually let the federal government grow in power and size. We have reached a critical point in our history. The current administration is attempting an enormous leap to a higher level of power and control. We are now seeing a concerted effort to speed up this process as President Obama's administration has increased the debt by trillions of dollars, raised the debt ceiling twice within the first sixteen months in office, and not allowed a budget to pass Congress since President Obama took office. If we sit back and let it happen we may never be able to regain our freedom again.

Imagine a pyramid of power representing the balance of power and control as it was set up by our founding fathers. It has a large, wide, and solid base representing the majority of power in the hands of the individual citizens. As we go up the pyramid, the power base becomes smaller for each level of government. Local government is smaller than the citizens, state government is smaller than local, and federal government is the smallest of all. This was the balance that was set up by our founding fathers. The intent was to leave as much power as possible in the hands of the citizens. It creates a solid, stable base that cannot be easily toppled by interest groups, world events, or economic turmoil.

Now imagine this pyramid turned upside down. The citizens at the bottom have a small amount of power, balanced on a tip that can easily be pushed over. Above the citizens is the weight of growing government control. Local, state, and federal government play an increasing role in controlling the citizens, who are being forced to support the growing weight of government. This pyramid is in danger of collapsing from the increasing weight at the top. It sways with every event and change. It is very unstable.

I believe we have been moving toward this upside down pyramid for some time. Since the 1930's, with the hardships of the depression opening the door for more government interference, the balance of power and control has been shifting toward the federal government. I believe these moves are heading us toward disaster with a balance of power that is very unstable economically and in direct opposition to the premise of maximum freedom for our citizens.

Our country promises equality. The equality of opportunity, not results. Our people are strong, inventive, hard-working and generous. We are individuals. We have different personalities, goals and talents. Some will get rich, some will become poor. The results are from our own choices. What we accomplish is our own responsibility. Government needs to step back, out of the way and let us get on with our own lives.

The liberal agenda will eventually fail, for they have no respect for the capabilities of individual citizens. The liberals think they are on the brink of total control. I believe they are on the brink of total collapse. They have gone too far and the people of this country like their independence.

At some point, enough citizens will realize the cost of government dependence is too high and cannot continue without eventual collapse. The question is how long will it take? How much damage will be done?

More of us are waking up and paying attention. We must continue to speak out and fight for the democracy we love. It will take hard work but Americans are very capable people. I have faith in our ability to succeed. The success of private citizens will offer the strongest economy, the most help for those in need, and the ability to retain our individual freedom.

Chapter 6
Who Do We Believe?

How do we judge who is telling the truth and who is misleading us? There is a constant barrage of noise in this "age of information". The liars are out there. They are taking full advantage of the sleeping public. The truth is also out there. How do we sort it all out?

Think of the commercials we see on TV. Talk about emotional appeal. I see so many that connect their product with something that tugs at our emotional heart strings or desires. A credit card company is running a commercial that shows how the small business entrepreneurs are bringing back America's economy. It is an emotional picture of Americans pulling themselves through the recession with hard work and creative thinking. There isn't a single word in the commercial about any advantage to using this particular credit card. It just makes the emotional connection to hard-working Americans.

There is a disturbing pattern of trying to solve problems from an emotional crisis mode. Our leaders often use a "we need to act now!" mentality. Unfortunately, this forces people to act quickly without time to think things through. Many mistakes are made and much damage can be done. It also offers enormous opportunity for people to take advantage of the situation for their own selfish profit.

When I woke up the rational side of my brain, I started thinking about what people were saying and questioning whether or not their claims were reasonable. The emotional appeal from politicians was no longer enough. I wanted to know the facts behind it.

I began to see disturbing patterns whenever liberal politicians and acquaintances were speaking. They spoke about issues with meaningless phrases. Like the ones that fit on bumper stickers. They spoke with great emotion. More emotion is supposed to indicate more sincerity. Many phrases they used were the same phrases I had heard 30 years ago.

Discussions often turned into raging monologues flinging accusations at conservatives and repeating catch phrases that I usually had heard several times the previous week from Democrat politicians.

This repetitive pattern makes me think there is some central control of the Democrat Party that has been building in recent years. It allows no deviation from the view or message of the week. It has pulled the party toward a radical, liberal position.

Of course, Democrats are not the only people who resort to this kind of communication. It seems, however, to be a deeply entrenched approach. It is officially embraced by the leaders of the Democrat Party to appeal and convince at an emotional level. This approach is also designed to dismiss and discourage logical discussion of issues.

Look at what happened to Joe Lieberman a few years back. He took a stand about the war in Iraq that did not follow the party line. The Democrat party proceeded to run another candidate against him trying to force him out. He had to run for re-election as an Independent to retain his congressional seat. I greatly admire his integrity and courage to stand up for what he believed, even though I disagree with some of his positions on other issues. I applaud the voters who re-elected him in spite of the efforts of the Democratic Party machine.

Some politicians have become more and more vicious in their attacks on their opponents (which is anyone who disagrees with them or even dares to question or ask for more information). There has been a growing trend in the liberal world to attack with name calling and unsubstantiated accusations rather than discuss or give supporting facts for their opinion on an issue.

In the 2008 election year the Democratic National Committee hired an expert to give advice to their candidates on how to get elected. I heard his advice was, "Tell people what makes them feel good." Never mind the facts. The truth doesn't matter. What a sad commentary on the American people and our gullibility.

It isn't just lies we have to look out for but distracting, useless information as well. Our brains are bombarded with constant input from radio, TV, computers, cell phones, text messaging, Twitter, and Facebook. The vast majority of it is useless information designed to entertain us, give us the illusion of connection to other people, convince us to buy a product, join a cause, or back a candidate.

We need to retrain ourselves to go beyond our initial emotional reaction and take time to sort out information, be skeptical, and ask questions. When it takes only a few sound bites to convince us we are probably reacting emotionally. If we stop there, we leave ourselves open to believing the wrong people and making bad decisions. We buy things we don't need. We choose friends or date people who bring us unhappiness. We are subject to the influence of others without any guiding principles of our own.

Asking questions is a powerful tool. Just to form a question requires us to think about the information. It opens the door to deeper understanding and sharing of information. Just receiving information isn't enough to bring understanding. It takes interaction, at least within our brain, to make a decision. Is this a good use of my time? Do I really need a new car? Is that job a good fit for me? Will that candidate make good decisions on my behalf? Asking questions of others creates discussion, real learning, and understanding.

I believe the most important skill we can learn and teach our children is how to sort out useful information from useless noise. There is no shortage of information. The noise keeps coming and unless we develop the ability to sort it out, it can easily overwhelm us to the point of total confusion. Only the loudest noise will get our attention. This is not a good measure of important information. Don't you just hate those loud commercials that blast you out of your seat with a volume set way above the program you were watching?

Every year I see students who love learning. They soak up information like sponges. It is amazing to see a child enter Kindergarten barely knowing the alphabet and in nine short months learn to read and write sentences. Such potential and enthusiasm!

Children reach a certain age where the emotionalism of adolescence takes over. The overwhelming feelings start to block out the thinking process. Any parent will attest to the frustration and lack of rational thought that comes out in conversations with teenagers. It is a natural progression in development. Most children will continue growing, maturing and learning. They will become mature adults with a balance of emotional and rational thought.

This maturity has to be carefully nourished by caring parents and teachers. Children need to be taught and have an opportunity to practice researching information, analyzing, questioning, discussing, compromising, solving problems, and being open to different points of view.

To sort out information and accurately analyze it, we must be willing to question all sources and opinions, including those we are inclined to believe. We must give respectful consideration and a degree of skepticism to all information and opinions that come our way. This is a balanced approach that allows thoughtful understanding of many sides of an issue. This is true open-mindedness. It allows us to benefit from the experiences and thoughts of others and to make decisions carefully.

Open-mindedness must be tempered with our values and principles. Each individual must develop a fundamental set of values and principles to use as a guide for life decisions. As a society, we must develop an agreed-upon set of values and principles to guide our shared future. They will limit confusion and clarify decisions. Without these values and principles to give us guidelines and limits, we descend into chaos. (I talk about values, principles, and character more in chapter 8.)

Which leaders do we believe? Who knows what the problems are and who can solve them? Who really wants to do what is best for our country? Certain patterns raise red flags in my mind when I listen to public figures.

Claims of crisis: When anyone claims we need to act immediately, I am suspicious. I want a clear definition of the crisis and its cause. I want to hear logical reasons for the necessity of acting immediately and I want a clear explanation of what steps are to be taken and why. If this additional information is not given, I believe the person doesn't know what they are talking about or they are trying to generate emotions of fear in the public for some selfish benefit.

Smoke screen information: Often, our leaders will give out a great deal of information that is of little or no importance. I wonder why they don't want us to pay attention to important issues. Why do they want us to be distracted?

Emotional tirades and name calling: This creates emotion to make the public feel a certain way about an issue or group of people. There is no useful information given. This person is unwilling or unable to debate issues, is trying to distract and deceive the public, and is unworthy of my trust.

Repeating phrases: Often, I hear several politicians saying the same phrase, almost word for word over the course of a week. Even when they are asked different questions, they find a way to work it into the response. I can only conclude that these sound bites have been handed out by the party leadership as a weekly agenda message. These phrases are designed to be heard over and over so the public will accept it as true. By having several people say it there is an illusion that it is a generally accepted fact.

No solutions offered: Many politicians will scream and yell about how wrong the opposition's actions are but never offer any reasonable solutions of their own. If someone doesn't offer specific solutions, they are wasting my time and I question their motivation.

We should listen to scientists, economists, businessmen, etc. who offer years of experience and solid evidence. Let's consider information that is given in a calm, thoughtful manner by people who back up their opinion with background information, sources, facts, and logical reasoning.

I have brought up the political scene in America because I believe the Democrat Party and liberal politics, in general, has become the vehicle of choice for those that want to take advantage of our sleeping brains. It is the ideal place to consolidate power, money and control. Emotional minds are easy to convince, control and ultimately rule. I believe the Democrat Party has refined its methods and agenda and wants to take control of government not through better solutions but by emotional appeal.

I wrote the above paragraphs before the 2008 presidential election results. The Democrats are now in charge of the presidency and have the majority in the Senate. Obviously, their emotional approach to the elections worked very well. (It worked again in 2012, but by a very narrow margin. Are more people waking up? I hope so.)

They are in a perfect position to keep the ball rolling. The parents and teachers who live by emotionalism have been teaching their children to get in touch with their feelings and leave reason sleeping. Those that can profit from this will continue to encourage the spread of the American coma.

Only the citizens can reverse the state of our country today. As long as we re-elect people who scream obscenities, call opponents names, and manipulate events, they will continue to act this way. As long as we buy products when an emotional or loud commercial runs, they will continue to run and give us very little information about the actual product.

We need to wake up and start using all of our brain power to deal with the world. Our decisions should be based on useful information, good judgment, and fundamental principles. Commercials will start giving us information about their product. Disagreements can once again become discussions that give birth to the best solutions. As citizens, we need to expect more civility, honesty, and common sense from our representatives and each other.

We need to pay attention all the time, not just during election cycles. We can sort through the noise. We can learn what questions to ask. As informed, rational consumers we will encourage useful information and discourage the emotional tricks. We will receive better products, better service, and a brighter future for ourselves and our children.

☜☞

Chapter 7
Heading Toward Socialism

I believe the United States is heading in the direction of socialism. It started with the panic of the 1930's depression. People were willing to dramatically change their view of government in order to "save" the country. The Federal Government gained unprecedented control over social programs and private business. People came to depend on the government for help.

Franklin Roosevelt was the only President elected for a third term. For over ten years, the country suffered with the depression. Roosevelt's approach seems to have been similar to President Obama's approach. Raise taxes on the rich and develop social programs for the needy. Take from those who have much and give it to those who have little. There is much debate about this approach.

We look back at the 1930's and see that the depression went on and on for over ten years. People were grateful to survive but they weren't thriving. The government approach did not improve the economy. Government programs did not create growth. They only transferred wealth by spending tax money. Many believe that it was only World War II that jump-started the economy with the sudden production demands and need for military personnel.

I am not an expert on the Depression but the resulting attitude change is clear. It became acceptable for the government to be more involved in the private business of citizens and for private citizens to depend on government help. Since that time, the Federal Government has gradually become bigger and bigger and become more involved in our daily lives. Now we expect the government to guarantee our savings accounts, force us to save for retirement with social security payments, replace our losses from disasters, give us funding for education, find another job for us, and pay for our healthcare. It goes on and on.

When changes happen gradually, we often don't notice how far they've gone. People scoff when the word socialism is mentioned but let's take a look at the dictionary's definition and see if we are closer to it than we realize.

"Socialism: A theory or system of social organization in which the means of production and distribution of goods are owned and controlled collectively or by the government 2. (in Marxist theory) the stage following capitalism in the transition of a society to communism, characterized by the imperfect implementation of collectivist principles.", *Random House Webster's College Dictionary*, 1997 edition.

Let's look carefully at what this definition means. The collective is always the government in a large society. Government owns/controls all businesses. The people controlling government decide what products are made, what services are provided, how much they will cost, who is eligible to receive them, how much will be produced.

Equity and Fairness are also decided by the government or state. They decide who gets that life saving operation, what your child is taught in school, where you can live, what kind of job you can have, and what information is allowed on the nightly news. If the government thinks you are making too much money at your job, they can lower your salary or raise your taxes and give it to someone else. The individual citizen has no voice in the matter. All aspects of life can be controlled by the government which supposedly represents the interest of the collective.

To keep citizens in compliance, children are educated (indoctrinated) by the state. Private citizens are not allowed to possess weapons or have any means of protest (such as free speech). No criticism of government is tolerated.

In a socialist system, a new class of people is given the exalted position of making decisions for the good of all citizens. The individual citizen has no value in this system. Accepting this new government ruling class requires a belief that somehow these chosen leaders are not subject to the weaknesses and temptations of human nature. We must believe that they will not abuse the immense power they have over citizens.

This is the downfall of any system that allows the few to rule the many. In spite of their own arrogance and ego these few are just human beings after all. They are just as motivated by self-interest as any other citizen. Inevitably, the government class will exempt themselves from many of the rules they impose on other citizens. Becoming a government official becomes the only way to obtain wealth and privilege.

Let's take a look at the activities of the Obama administration. There has been a clear pattern of increased control by the executive branch. The President and his staff have been very involved in controlling banks, private businesses, radio, television, the internet, healthcare, and education. They have found ways to bypass Congress using increased regulations and presidential decrees.

Financial institutions have been highly regulated for many years. Citing the economic crisis and using stimulus money, the Obama administration gained an ownership interest in some banks. Anytime the government gives out money it has "control" strings attached. Banks were told that the government would do a "stress test" on any bank it chose and dictate how the banks should be run. The government has been making up new rules as it pleases and forcing banks to "borrow" money and be under their control.

Some banks tried to return the money after realizing they were better off working out their problems themselves. The government wouldn't let them return the money! (Note: In December, 2009, Wells Fargo was finally allowed to return borrowed money. I haven't heard the details of what was required by the Federal Government to allow the return.)

The Federal Government now controls 100% of all student loans to college students. How much control do they have on what is taught to our students in college? This is a legitimate question particularly after hearing some of the teaching methods by college professors that have come to light in recent years. We should be concerned about whether our students are being educated to think for themselves or brainwashed to think like their professors and their benefactor, the federal government.

The automobile industry has certainly been in the news lately. When large private industries experience financial problems, the acceptable solution is to let government step in, use our tax money to bail them out and control how the companies are run.

None of this government interference is necessary. When a private business is in trouble we have bankruptcy laws that are designed to help companies deal with their creditors fairly and if possible be reorganized to become a successful company again.

On the other end of the spectrum, large companies that are doing very well are brought under government scrutiny. Oil companies, Walmart, and company executives who earn large bonuses have been vilified by the Federal Government. Political leaders have promoted the notion that we should punish those who are making too much money. They want to control profit and promote emotional class warfare. Government control is becoming the accepted answer for every problem or inequity.

I've heard talk that the FCC wants to control the content of radio talk shows by resurrecting the "Fairness Doctrine". Most of the media doesn't even mention it.

In recent years, conservative talk radio has become very popular. The number of shows and the number of listeners is rapidly increasing. There seems to be a desire to control the content of these shows by the Obama administration.

Over the years, government has controlled radio and television with licensing and regulations. If you don't follow the rules, the government yanks your license. This is the kind of behind-the-scenes control that most of us don't pay much attention to, but we should.

It isn't that hard to gradually increase control until there is total censorship. It has happened in many countries. It is always disguised as for the public good but it can so easily step over the line to infringe on freedom of speech and exert government control of information.

Healthcare has become another government control issue. The idea of nationalized healthcare has been promoted for many years. Let's be clear. This is government control of your health and one sixth of the economy. Government officials and bureaucrats will make medical decisions about what medication and procedures you will be allowed to have. They will have the power to override medical decisions by doctors.

The next logical step after increasing control is actual ownership. It should not be surprising that the current administration has started taking ownership interest in "troubled" companies.

People will argue that if we have an elected government then the will of the citizens is still represented. The problem is when you give government officials more control it is easier for them to change the rules and ensure that voting goes their way. They can control what your children are taught in school, what information is released or kept hidden from the public, and what radio and television stations will have their licenses renewed.

Remember the terrorist attack in Libya? The Obama administration deliberately misled the public about what happened until after the 2012 election. They didn't just withhold information, they spread a story about a video and spontaneous protests that they knew wasn't true. The president himself told this story in front of the UN. We now know that the administration knew it was a coordinated terrorist attack as it was happening. For six hours, they watched video from a drone as our people were attacked and killed. They sent no help. They made up a lie. All this was done to influence the outcome of the election.

Now that Obama has been reelected for a second term (2012), over 6,000 new regulations are scheduled to go into effect over the next few months. Many changes are behind the scenes, many are gradual and most of us are unaware of them unless we are paying attention and asking questions. These regulations are put into action with no public discussion. They provide a huge opportunity for government to control more and more of our society without any awareness by citizens. That is, until prices increase. By then, of course, government will be able to blame greedy big business.

We need to know more about what goes on behind the scenes. Press conferences and speeches give us very little information about what the government is really doing. It takes some effort on our part but we need to seek out a variety of news sources to get a more detailed picture.

For years, we have seen reinterpretation of the Constitution become an accepted practice. These changes may seem unimportant by themselves but they can lead to changing our country beyond recognition.

There is an increasing concentration of power behind the scenes with Presidential decrees and appointed commissions, directors and "czars" that bypass the checks and balances of our three branches of federal government and the accountability of elections.

President Obama has publicly stated while signing a new law that he didn't like the law and did not intend to enforce it. He is putting his own wishes first and is refusing to abide by the rule of law (which is the responsibility of every citizen) and is declaring his intent not to enforce certain laws (which is his sworn oath of office duty). He is putting himself above the law.

Recently, President Obama issued a proclamation regarding illegal immigrants that have completed high school in the United States. He has, in fact, issued orders to the INS (Immigration and Naturalization Service) to ask any suspected illegal alien if they have completed high school. The agents are not allowed to ask for any proof. If the illegal alien says yes they have to release them with no further questions. INS agents have even been ordered to release illegal aliens who are being held for violent crimes. Agents have been speaking out. This is the reality of a seemingly harmless proclamation.

Without debating the wisdom of this proclamation, it is important to note that the President does not have the power to change immigration laws. Only the Congress has that power, per the Constitution. He is acting outside the legal limits of his office.

The Congress has been passing the President's bills without even reading them. Procedure rules have been changed to eliminate discussion by opposing congressmen and senators. It is amazing that so many congressmen are giving up so much of their own power without protest.

The liberal leaders think they are ushering in a new age. It is, despite all their pretty speeches, an old idea. It has been tried over and over all around the world and all through history. A few people with enormous arrogance believe they have the right to tell the rest of us what to do. Any method is justified because the end will be their vision of the ideal society (the vision always includes them being in charge). The anointed few will rule the many. Socialism, Communism, Dictatorships all come about from this arrogance.

I believe we have reached a crossroads in the history of our country. The believers of the socialist ideology are enjoying "a perfect wave". They have spent years influencing public opinion, creating or exaggerating crisis issues, and pushing for more government programs. After gaining more and more control of the media, schools, courts, Congress, and the Presidency the timing couldn't be better to turn our democracy into a socialist society.

President Obama himself has openly stated his goals to establish nationalized healthcare and redistribute wealth.

He tells the disenfranchised he is with them. He encourages rich versus poor class warfare, while he takes large donations for his campaign and has quite a bit of money himself.

The sacrifices citizens will be forced to make will not apply to government workers. They have their own health care program, retirement system and pay scales. Remember, the government is the new privileged class.

President Obama has enlarged or prolonged various crisis situations. The explosion of one oil platform turned into a complete shutdown of all oil rigs in the Gulf which put the Gulf States into a huge economic crisis. He pulls out support of the military, and makes anti-business remarks. He degrades individual accomplishment, encourages violent demonstrations by the occupy movement, and offers more government interference as the only solution to problems.

The conditions are right, people are motivated. If the citizens of the United States do not wake up and put on the brakes, a transformation to socialism could happen fast!

President Obama's actions are a realization of Saul Alinsky's "Rules for Radicals" playbook and classic

Marxist methods: exaggerate every crisis, encourage unrest, play groups against each other, ridicule religious beliefs, dismiss the value of individual accomplishment, give financial favors to those who support you, demonize those who oppose or even question you (never argue the actual issue), seize more control over information outlets and private business, increase executive power, disarm the public, convince citizens that government control is the only way to solve problems.

Hugo Chavez took Venezuela from a democracy to a socialist dictatorship in only ten years. It can happen here if we are not paying attention.

Will it work? Will our lives be better? Will everyone have all they need? There are many people who believe it would improve our lives. Unfortunately, they have been proved wrong many times.

The socialist system has been tried before in many forms. It usually starts with a particular problem or crisis. Sometimes, a revolution takes place and a new government is formed. Sometimes, it isn't that dramatic or sudden. An existing government can gradually move toward a socialist system.

There are people in the United States, including members of our government, who believe this is the direction our country should go. They have been diligently working toward this goal for years, gaining more power and control for government one issue at a time. Some truly have good intentions and believe it would create an ideal world for everyone. Others encourage the movement because they are clever enough to take advantage of it for their own selfish goals.

No matter what the motivation, a socialist society is doomed to failure. It has always failed in the past and will fail in the future. It will fail because the socialist theory has a fatal flaw. It does not acknowledge human nature. It does not reflect an understanding of the basic motivations of human beings. No matter how much someone thinks their system will work, unless they have accepted and understand the basic nature of people, they will never succeed. The socialists may get control for awhile but ultimately they will cause great damage and will have to admit defeat.

People are first motivated to survive. Survival of self and offspring is built into every living animal. Humans are no exception. People will endure incredible hardships to survive and protect their family. If everything else is taken away, survival is the prime directive.

Survival alone, however, isn't enough for humans. What separates us from the other animals is awareness of not only the environment around us but what is beyond us. Most of us believe in a Creator. All of us have some understanding of the universe beyond our own experience. We have a spark in us that motivates us to look beyond mere survival and strive to seek knowledge, invent, build, improve, and share.

People want a better life for themselves and their families. The definition of a better life is unique to the individual but there are common motivations. We want to be rewarded for our hard work. We want to feel something belongs to us. We want our individuality to show in our lives.

This individuality must be acknowledged and valued by any system of government in order to succeed. This is where the socialist system fails. When a socialist system insists that no matter how hard you work, you should have the same two bedroom apartment that everyone else has, people lose the incentive to work hard, to invent, to improve. There is no reward for accomplishment.

Gradually, productivity starts declining with fewer and fewer people producing to support more and more non-producing people. The economy will start to fail. There will be shortages of goods, fewer and fewer jobs and eventually a total collapse of the society.

People will abandon the government system as much as possible, developing a black-market buying, selling, and trading system to replace the official economy. For many, it will be the only way they can survive. Crime will rise as people become more desperate. Eventually, the people will demand a change.

My grandparents came from Poland. Through the years of Soviet rule, their relatives related how bad conditions became in their country. Even if they had money, there was nothing to buy in the stores.

The other part of human nature is the human condition. Humans can be selfish, dishonest, and violent. We have free will and people make different choices. This part of our nature must also be acknowledged by any successful system of government.

While allowing the individual's freedom, we must also have safeguards to protect others. Allowing a few to rule the many takes away safeguards and gives tremendous power to a few who can misuse it for selfish goals.

Understanding the full potential of humans, both positive and negative, our founding fathers created a form of government that gives the individual the maximum individual freedom while insuring public safety. It limits the power of our leaders with checks and balances between the branches of government.

They declared inalienable rights of life, liberty and the pursuit of happiness given by God, (or by nature, if you prefer), to make sure everyone understood that no man, however powerful, could be justified in taking away these rights from others.

They established the rule of law under which we all, from the poorest to the richest, powerless to powerful, must live. We have equal protection under the law, equal opportunity to pursue our dreams.

They established a free market economy which allows businesses to succeed or fail based on consumer power. If the demand is high, the supply will have a market and the business will flourish. If demand is low, a business is badly managed or can't survive competition, it will fail.

When the supply and demand rules of the free market work with a minimum of interference from government, it creates a solid economy that reacts to the power of the consumer. Every product and service is designed to please the consumer. Businesses are motivated to keep finding ways to offer the best product, the best service, and the lowest possible price.

Unfortunately, our government has a history of "tinkering" with our economy. Failing businesses are propped up and healthy businesses are regulated or taxed out of business. All this creates an artificial economy which can't always react in balance with market forces.

The only beneficiary of this is government itself. They can increase their power by promising to fix the problems they themselves have created. They may succeed in creating a short-term fix which looks good on their watch but it will cause more problems in the long run.

We must encourage our government to go back to the basic principles of our free market democracy. We need less interference from government, not more.

The balanced system that our founding fathers created has worked very well. It allowed this country to become a strong, vibrant, generous leader in the world. It allowed independent citizens to build better lives for themselves and their families. People poured into this country from all over the world because it offered the best opportunity for individual accomplishment.

We need to renew our enthusiasm and ambition, and embrace again the principles of our founding fathers. We need to again believe that we are in charge of our own destiny, responsible for our lives, and the direction of our country.

We must move forward correcting mistakes of the past, gaining more understanding of the world, but keeping our principles intact to empower every individual.

No matter who wins an election, it is only the will of the people that will make lasting changes. We must educate ourselves and our children. We must have a clear vision of our principles and keep an alert, watchful eye on the representatives we elect. Our founding principles along with our individual principles should be the framework used to measure all decisions we face.

Chapter 8
The Character of America

What is the character of America? What kind of people are we? What are our values and principles? Do we have a clear vision of our common goals? Are we focused on achieving them? Are our shared values, principles, and goals reflected and encouraged by our government? Is the direction of our country what we believe is best for us and others? We need to answer all these questions in order to choose the direction of our future.

So much emphasis today is put on celebrating our differences. We need to respect and value individuality and our heritage but we need to celebrate what we all have in common, as well. What we have in common allows us to live day to day with each other to the mutual benefit of all.

The common bonds of our national character define us and determine our future as a nation. If there is a disconnect between the people and the government, it is the duty of the citizens to bring government back in line to reflect and support our shared values. If various groups of people are at odds with each other they need to go back to basic common values and principles to work out a compromise.

It is the hope and goal of democracy to have the maximum individual freedom while functioning as a cohesive society. To achieve this we, as individuals, must clarify our own values and principles. This is the foundation upon which we judge right and wrong, what helps or harms us, what direction we want our lives to take.

However, the individual is not isolated. Our values are formed and work in the context of our families, communities, countries, and world. We are part of a whole. In order for the whole to function, each individual must cooperate, contribute, and compromise. We may hold values that others don't share but there must be a level of mutual agreement that keeps our society working.

When we have a period of change, as in the last fifty years, it causes a fractured society. Citizens try living by new rules, discarding established values. Often many groups with conflicting ideas are trying to change society at the same time. These transitional stages of society can be dangerous. If we go too far asserting the individual's right to do anything, we have chaos. If we go too far asserting the society's right to control everything, we have tyranny.

One of the unique challenges for America is that we have citizens from all over the world with different cultural and family histories. Yet, we must all agree upon common values and principles that hold us together and create the American identity.

If we can manage to hold onto a unified American Identity, the diversity of our citizens is our greatest asset. Many ideas are better than one. The creativity of shared ideas brings forth great achievement.

If we do not maintain a common set of values and goals, our diversity tears us apart. Individual, selfish goals overpower our pledge to act responsibly for the common good.

Some will argue that our society is changing and we must reinvent the wheel over and over. This was certainly the attitude of the young in the 1960's and continues today.

I believe there are certain values and principles that are the foundation to all human societies. They have stood the test of various cultures and time. No matter what changes occur, the human being is essentially the same. We have the same basic needs, strengths, and weaknesses. The same principles allow us to build civilizations and the same problems cause civilizations to fall.

These positive values and principles have common characteristics. They promote achievement and contribution. They cause action that considers the welfare of others in balance with self-interest. Since they require a person to think beyond themselves and the moment, they need to be taught, practiced, and encouraged to become part of an individual's character. When these values and principles are consistently taught, they remain the foundation of our American character.

Honesty:

I was raised in a family where honesty was very important. My parents were good examples. If someone gave us too much change in a store, we gave it back. If a child had reached an age where the admission price had increased my parents never lied to save money (and they were counting pennies). The only exception was in situations where someone would be hurt and nothing would be accomplished. Sometimes, rushing to tell the "truth" can cause needless pain.

Out in the world, I have come across many people who are not honest. Some seem to be rewarded for lying, at least, in the short term. I still feel that honesty is best for all concerned. The person who lies diminishes their own character and usually makes their own life much more complicated. The harm to others varies but would the world be better if everybody lied or if everybody told the truth?

The importance of honesty goes beyond individuals. We see the damage in money lost, people hurt, lives lost by dishonest people in our world. Lying is a sure sign that someone is acting in self-interest, not thinking of what's best for others.

There will always be some who are dishonest. It is part of the human condition. It is part of the reason government is necessary at all. However, if honesty is clearly encouraged and valued by a society, it makes a difference. It prevents dishonesty from becoming widespread and acceptable.

Does our government encourage honesty? Well, they certainly insist that our tax return be accurate! Sadly, I don't know anyone who would characterize politicians as honest. An honest politician seems to be the exception to the rule. Many speeches by politicians are meant to confuse, mislead and outright lie to the public in order to protect and promote the politician's agenda. Some justify lying as a necessary means to a noble end. I can't buy it, though. If you can't convince people that you know what to do by telling the truth, then something is wrong with your idea or your opinion of the public. It usually reflects an arrogant attitude.

Any parent will tell you, children pay attention to what we do not just what we say. Our politicians need to greatly improve in this area. When they are evasive or untruthful, we, as responsible citizens, need to challenge them and insist on being told the truth. Our children need to be taught the importance of honesty and people in the public eye as well as parents should be good examples.

Kindness and generosity: Kindness toward others is a quality that is often overlooked. I believe it is the most important quality of all. It embodies the "thinking of others" frame of mind. I am treading on the emotional side of the brain a little. After all, we need a balance of emotion and rational thought. Kindness and generosity is a perfect way to show that balance.

Emotions developed to feel empathy, understanding, and sympathy lead us to feel a desire to be kind. Our rational thinking helps us turn kind feelings into acts of generosity. It helps us figure out what we can do to make someone feel better and what help they really need to get on their feet again.

Sometimes, when people are trying to be "kind" from a solely emotional point of view it can be harmful rather than a help to others. Being "kind" to someone to the point of making them totally dependent can cause great harm. Often referred to as, "smother love", kindness ends up making the giver feel good but can damage the receiver's ability to be independent, grow and learn new skills. Their self-image can be damaged by someone who thinks they are showing kindness, when in fact, they are feeding their own ego and giving the underlying message that someone else is less capable. The "I know what's best for you" attitude can grow into an "I know better than you" attitude. Many political leaders slip into this arrogant attitude. Their quest for the world they want justifies all sorts of harmful actions. The "I know better than you" attitude leads to a distain for others, with no merit given to their ideas and opinions. Sometimes the original goal of helping people is completely forgotten as the pursuit of money, power, and control becomes all-consuming.

Maintaining the dignity and self-respect of another person is true kindness. This is often done quietly, privately, and without saying "Look what I've done!" to others.

I sometimes feel insulted when I hear politicians yelling that we need more government programs to help people. Do they think only government helps those in need? The American people are the most generous in the world. We donate more money, time and effort to charity and relief programs than any other country.

Can government programs reflect our nation's kindness? Perhaps they can, if they have very specific goals and are carefully watched. Large disasters often require immense efforts. The large resources of government may be necessary on a temporary basis.

In most cases, I believe the best help comes from family and community. Help on these levels is individualized and personal. As organizations and government agencies get larger the help becomes more of a, "one size fits all", help with more and more restrictions for eligibility. These organizations are often not efficient or accommodating to the individual.

As a college student, I considered becoming a social worker. I went to the local county family aid office and spent the day sitting and observing from the client's point of view. Most of the clients were women, often with young children in tow. They sat in hard plastic chairs for hours, trying to quiet bored, crying children. The entire room was filled with an atmosphere of defeat. Conversations with clerks and social workers seemed full of frustration and focused on the reason help was being denied. The government workers didn't seem very friendly or even polite.

Talking with social workers revealed they were overloaded with work and frustration. They were caught in the middle. People were desperate for help but the system was so mired in regulations and restrictions that the help was often not available. That one day convinced me to look for another career. I became a teacher, enjoying the hopeful and enthusiastic world of children.

In contrast, I have visited local shelters, community food banks, and church outreach programs. The atmosphere was completely different. There was an atmosphere of hope and caring. I saw people laughing and visiting. Those who came to be helped and those who helped were one community. People were welcomed and treated with respect and kindness.

Strength, Patience, Perseverance: These three qualities help us through the tough times. They enable us to continue working hard toward a goal even when the goal is not close at hand. These qualities are a must for research scientists searching for a cure, someone who has been injured and is trying to walk again, training for the Olympics, or finishing years of education to qualify for a career. There is no instant gratification to real accomplishment. It takes emotional desire and rational thought to keep us going, to see the purpose to our far-reaching goals, to understand what it takes to go step-by-step toward that goal.

Our country certainly has a history of these qualities. Are we still encouraging and developing these traits in our children? In a world of so many instant gratifications, we need to help our children set long-term goals and experience the satisfaction of reaching them.

Creativity, Independence, and Courage: These are the qualities of people who think for themselves. These people do not just blindly follow the crowd. They are brave enough to go out on their own, to stand up for what they believe. These are the people who invent, start new businesses, protect our country, and give more to the world than they take.

It took all of those qualities to create our unique country. People from all over the world have come to the United States to pursue their dreams. They come for the promise of freedom and opportunity. They leave everything behind to seek something better. They come believing that great things can be achieved.

We need this spirit to move forward in our country. I believe it is alive and well among our citizens. However, there are elements of discouragement in our leaders. There has been a growing trend to encourage dependency and to stifle creativity and courage. This makes people believe that they can't accomplish anything without the help of government. This encourages a "passive sheep" attitude and can only help government gain more control.

Hard Work and Responsibility: These qualities have traditionally been held in high regard. Hard work is what gets us, step-by-step, to our goals. Figuring out how to work smart can make things easier but taking short cuts can be tricky. Young adults who expect to get a high-paying, prestigious job right out of school are not being realistic. Disappointment can lead to blaming others, losing hope, giving up, or throwing some values aside to "short-cut" the system.Taking responsibility for our lives lets us rethink, adjust, and seek more knowledge. We take the action to improve our own lives. This puts the work on us but it gives us the power and control over the direction of our lives. Responsibility is the ultimate freedom!

Does our society embrace hard work and responsibility? The accomplishments of this country have been the envy of the world. When my grandparents emigrated from Poland, they were willing and expected to work hard to achieve their dreams.

Today, many people who are hardworking and responsible have a curious acceptance of irresponsibility on the part of others. This is reflected in the type of social programs we are funding. Some programs give people food or a place to live but don't help them become self-sufficient again. Other programs let people buy homes they can't afford which ultimately leads to financial ruin. When we take away the pride of earning our own way the incentive to put out the effort, be responsible, and be independent starts to diminish. To be taken care of becomes expected and acceptable.

As a society, we have become more accepting of excuses for unacceptable behavior. This leads to the attitude that others are responsible for the problems in our lives. We need to remind ourselves and teach our children that we each have control of our own lives if we accept the responsibility and are willing to work to reach our goals.

Is hard work and responsibility being encouraged by our government? Are citizens rewarded or are they punished with higher taxes? If we continue to expand the idea of taking from the rich and giving to the poor, we are really discouraging hard work, responsibility and success.

We should help those who aren't capable of working or taking responsibility. But should we also help those who make bad decisions, buy things they can't afford, or continue to live destructive lives? Should help come from private sources, local governments or federal programs? No matter what the source of help, the emphasis should always be to keep as much independence and responsibility in the hands of the individual as possible.

Honesty, kindness, generosity, strength, patience, perseverance, creativity, independence, courage, hard work, and responsibility: The American Character has been defined by these values and principles from our founding. We must continue to embrace, encourage, and teach them to keep our country growing toward a positive future. We must elect politicians who embody these values and principles, act as role models for our children, and encourage our government to reflect the character of our citizens. This America will encourage our citizens to pursue their dreams.

Chapter 9
Waking Up America

How do we wake up from the American Coma? This condition has been spreading across our nation for over 50 years! The emotional brain approach has gradually become ingrained in every part of our lives and every level of government.

The dangers are many and they are growing larger. Emotional decisions are causing us to do harm to ourselves and others. We are easy targets to be manipulated by self-serving con artists. It is allowing forces in politics to pull us toward total dependence on government. It is encouraging violent forces around the world to act against us when they see no firm resolve to fight them.

The dangers of letting emotions run our lives should be a call to action. We need to be fully alert and actively engaged in what is happening around us. Those of us who have been quiet yet worried need to speak out.

Sharing rational thoughts and ideas will influence emotional minds. It happened to me!

I go back to my own experience as a "sleeping mind". It happened little by little over time. I remember a discussion about Rush Limbaugh with co-workers. Most of us were dismissive of him, although I doubt any of us had heard even one entire program. However, one young secretary was defending him.

She said she listened to his program and found what he said interesting. It made her think about issues and she actually agreed with many of the things he said.

She was a very likeable person. I enjoyed talking to her. She wasn't confrontational. She didn't insist she was right or that someone else was wrong. She just offered her opinion with a smile. The other co-workers continued to make snide remarks about Rush. That bothered me.

I listened to her and later thought about what she said. I sought out Rush Limbaugh on the radio and started listening. I had heard a few bits and pieces from his show in the past and I thought he was a loud, brash know-it-all with a huge ego. This was the impression my liberal friends expressed as well.

As I listened to Rush a little more, however, something began to happen. I began to think about things he said. I began to see the sense in things he said. I understood his sense of humor and the necessity for having a little showmanship to entertain his listeners.

Gradually, I tuned my radio to other talk shows. My husband has always been interested in science and liked listening to Bill Wattenburg. I began to listen along with him. Listening to a well-respected scientist exposed me to logic and evidence-based conclusions.

His opinions were developed over time with experience and fact-based knowledge.

My husband has been a big influence on me. He has always looked at issues beyond the surface. He asks questions (sometimes to the point of being annoying) about everything. He has an uncanny ability to find solutions while others are still scratching their heads. He thinks about cause and effect, quietly observes and analyzes before he makes decisions. He is a long-term thinker. I've been lucky to have such a good example of logical thinking by my side.

Influencing others requires that we take stock of our own approach to life. The call to action must first begin with self examination. Once we have clarified our own positions, we can then present a focused point of view and direction to others.

Embrace Responsibility: Once we take responsibility, we realize the freedom of choice is ours. It doesn't mean we will never have difficulties. Life does not come with guarantees. What we will have is the power to change our lives, to choose our direction and goals. We can take action ourselves, not wait for others to change things for us.

If we become dependent on others we give up our freedom of choice. If someone else has the responsibility, they also have the control. Blaming others for our problems means we are powerless to solve them. I don't think any of us know many people we would trust to have total control of our lives. Why are so many people willing to surrender their responsibility and thereby lose control of their lives to total strangers in government?

Clarify Our Values and Principles: Each individual needs a clear set of values and principles to guide their actions. It is helpful to review them occasionally, to remind ourselves of what is important and to renew our focus on the direction of our lives.

These individual values and principles form the building blocks for the values and principles of our society. We can make decisions with clarity if we remember to go back to our basic principles whenever we are confused. Political decisions should be made the same way. A personal review should include some review of our society as well. Are our country's actions compatible with our principles? If not, perhaps we should spend a little time gathering information, questioning and speaking up about actions that are taking us off course.

The basic principles our founding fathers used to set up the checks and balances structure of our government have worked very well. Our history is not perfect but our government structure and free market system is by far the most successful in the world—ever!

We have the advantage of looking back at history. We can learn from our past mistakes and successes and those of others. We can continue to improve our country and help other nations as well. Using our present knowledge without abandoning our founding principles will lead us to a balanced future full of opportunity.

Develop An Open Mind: We need to develop an open mind and respect for the ideas of others. At the same time, we need a healthy skepticism that allows us to ask questions and watch for red flags from all sources, even ones we tend to trust. This allows us to make decisions about the validity of all information. An open mind has to be periodically reviewed. We tend to settle into a mind set that becomes comfortable. Being comfortable can lead to a closed mind, unwilling to listen and consider new ideas and unwilling to question old ideas or sources. Personal growth is a life-long process. We will never know everything but we can always learn more.

Judging Information: Making a judgment about the usefulness, quality, and truthfulness of information is crucial to living in this information age. We need to be aware and informed consumers. Glitzy commercials may be amusing and get our attention but they should not determine whether or not we buy a product. Politicians make wonderful speeches with many promises and emotional phrases but questions should be asked. A man may be very romantic but will he be a good and faithful husband?

Anytime information comes our way the first step is deciding if the information is useful to us. The vast majority of "noise" is not useful, only distracting. It takes practiced skill to discard all the useless and focus on the useful and important information. It takes all the skill our emotional and rational brain can muster.

From babyhood on, we take in information and start analyzing, sorting, and learning appropriate responses. As we get older, the information, messages, and clues become more numerous and complicated. Our response to the information needs to become more complicated, too. When we are very young, emotional reactions suffice for our basic needs. Crying will get us changed or a bottle or a comforting hug. As we get older, however, our responses need to involve more rational thought.

The information age is upon us. The question is can we make sense of it? Our values and principles will be our guide.

Teach Our Children: The only way to achieve lasting change in a society is to teach and encourage children. Many adults assume that at a certain age, children will automatically start taking responsibility for their actions. They will develop the skills of rational thought, problem solving, and long-term thinking. They will become well-balanced, capable adults. They have forgotten their own childhood and development into adulthood.

Children need the guidance and example of adults. Becoming a fully developed, well-balanced adult requires learning and practicing a wide range of skills. We need to teach our children the skills of rational thought, the process of scientific methods, the value of evidence and various opinions. This isn't easy when the world around them is flying by the seat of their emotional pants. Parents have a great influence on their children. Even when they reach the teenage years our input still sinks in. Initial reactions and peer influence should not cause us to give up. Loving, caring guidance from adults who know them will make a difference.

Pay attention to what schools are teaching your children. You can ask individual teachers what thinking skills are being taught at that grade level, you can talk to principals, district personnel and school board members. Ask your children questions about their school day and listen carefully to what they say. Make an appointment to come and observe your child's class.

As students progress through grade levels, higher level thinking skills should be part of the lessons. There should be opportunity and encouragement to:
- express differing opinions, not just follow the teacher's opinion
- gather and analyze information
- practice using rational, logical, and linear thought
- develop skills to sort, prioritize, make judgments, and solve problems

Beware of teachers who express their own emotion-based views as "fact" to their students. This is not appropriate and is happening all too often in schools across the country. Students are impressionable and teachers have a responsibility to teach skills that allow students to develop their own ability to form opinions. If we have an issue with what is being taught to our children we have a duty to speak up.

One of the important foundations of the Communist System is state run public education. The government can then control what information, what beliefs, what values are instilled in children. To avoid this danger, citizens, especially parents, need to be aware and involved. There are good reasons that private school options have been increasing popular in recent years. Parents want choices and a voice in what their children are taught.

Share Rational Thought: As I started listening to more sources, it led to questioning, looking for more information and eventually changing some of my opinions. I believe those who have rational ideas need to keep sharing them. In spite of an initial negative response, people often think about things later.

We don't have to be shouting at people or making grand speeches. Inserting a question or an idea into a one-on-one conversation can be very effective. We can express our views in a calm and respectful manner. Challenging, emotional, and in-your-face rhetoric causes people to put up protective barriers, unless they already agree with you. The young lady in my office who offered her opinion with a quiet voice and a big smile will never know the impact she had on my thinking. Patience and persistence will pay off eventually.

Use Our Consumer Power: To accomplish change beyond our own circle of self, family, and friends we need to assert our consumer power in all aspects of public life. We need our developed values, principles, and rational decisions to reflect in what we are buying. This is the ultimate power of the people.

The consumer has the power to change the quality of products and services that are offered. Whether we are dealing with schools, private companies, radio and TV stations, newspapers and magazines, or government our voices can be heard. It is up to us to get involved and speak up. When the free market is allowed to work, the needs and wishes of the people will be reflected in the products and services offered.

Since our consumer power in government is expressed by voting, change takes time and persistence. There are many things we can do between elections to make politicians aware of our views. Writing letters, sending e-mails, making phone calls, and participating in town hall meetings, are all ways to send a consumer message. We each must decide what actions are right for us. Sending just one letter can make a difference.

Chapter 10
Hope for the Future

I have great hope for our future. I see many people, just like me, waking up their rational brain. They are thinking, asking questions, and speaking out.

The wonderful thing about human beings is the ability to learn not only from our own experiences but from the experiences of others. The ability to learn through communication not just direct experience gives us the unique opportunity to change our environment not just cope with it. This gives us great power and, therefore, great responsibility.

We have the responsibility to make good decisions by developing our thinking skills so we know what questions to ask, and how to determine the sources and quality of information we receive. Is the source of information interested in our welfare or just self-serving? Are they well-informed? What are the sources of their "facts"? Does the quality of the information make it worth listening to or believable?

We need to develop sensitivity for the "red flags" in life. It keeps us safe, helps us avoid dangerous situations. It helps us determine what is true and what is not.

Rational facts and ideas do have an effect on the emotional mind. The challenge is to make the rational information available to the public. People are capable of learning, growing, and maturing no matter what their age or experience. One conversation can start someone on the road to thinking and asking questions. That's all it takes.

The pendulum of social trends swings back and forth. Nature always searches for the balance. Humans are no exception. We function best when emotional and rational thought are used together to decide our actions.

It's time for ordinary citizens to become more active. Let's take responsibility for our own lives and teach our children the skills to shape their own destiny. Let's listen to different opinions, ask questions, speak up, and participate in our democracy.

We are so fortunate to live in the United States. Our choices are endless. Opportunities are abundant. We take it for granted. We are easily lulled into complacency. We must constantly remind ourselves how unique our freedom is in the world.

We must be alert to the dangers in life. There are many threats to the safety of our personal lives and our society. In this world there are people who will do anything to gain money, power, and control. They will lie, steal, and violently take with force what people do not give willingly. History is full of horrible examples.

The conmen have endless tricks to convince us that we need their "help". They prey on the weak and vulnerable. They create class envy, focus blame on the innocent, and foment fear and hate.

We must be constantly vigilant for those who put themselves above us, insisting we must believe as they do, and claiming they have the right to decide what's best for us. Our freedom can be gone in the blink of an eye if we stay asleep. So we must be fully awake, all of our brain engaged.

In this great country, I can worship God in the church of my choice (or not), choose my line of work, live where I want, and speak my mind.

I meet so many wonderful people who work hard, give generously, and quietly make the world a better place. They inspire me every day. We are a country of creativity, courage, and hope.

We citizens are the ultimate power of this country. We have the final say if we exercise it. No matter where we are, we can take that next step toward a better life. So wake up America! Enjoy the abundance of freedom and protect it for our children.

Recommended Information Sources

Radio Talk Shows–A great variety of opinions abound. Keep in mind the red flags discussed in chapter 6 when listening to any talk show host. My favorite station in the San Francisco Bay Area is KSFO. Hosts like Barbara Simpson, Brian Sussman, Melody Morgan, Mike Huckabee, Michael Savage, Sean Hannity, Rush Limbaugh, and Mark Levin present opinions and discussions of issues that are often not covered in mainstream news.

Cable TV News–Most news shows cover or don't cover stories according to their own political agenda. Watching a variety of news shows gives me a more balanced picture of the world. I like the Fox News Channel as a counterbalance to network TV news.

The Heritage Foundation–This is a think tank in Washington DC. They provide an historical and rational perspective on current issues. You can become a member and receive many opinion pieces by some of the leading scholars in our country. Check out their website at heritage.org

Hillsdale College–A college that accepts no government funds. They offer free on-line courses on the Constitution and U.S. History. Each lecture is given by various professors from the college. They are very interesting and informative. Their website is hillsdale. edu